IMAGES
of America

BADLANDS
NATIONAL PARK

The Badland's breathtaking formations appear as if they are composed of solid rock. Actually, they are mudstones, claystones, and siltstones that seem like rock but disintegrate in water

IMAGES
of America

BADLANDS
NATIONAL PARK

Jan Cerney

ARCADIA
PUBLISHING

Published by Arcadia Publishing
Charleston, South Carolina

Printed in the United States of America

Library of Congress Catalog Card Number: 2003113879

For all general information contact Arcadia Publishing at:
Telephone 843-853-2070
Fax 843-853-0044
E-mail sales@arcadiapublishing.com
For customer service and orders:
Toll-Free 1-888-313-2665

Visit us on the Internet at www.arcadiapublishing.com

For centuries erosion has whittled away sediments collected during millions of years of geological changes. The magical chisels of wind and rain have created magnificent sculptures, each unique in appearance and design.

CONTENTS

ACKNOWLEDGMENTS

I am very grateful to the Badlands National Park for giving me the opportunity to use the Park's extensive photograph collection. Without the commitment to preserving history, this book would not have been possible. Thank you to all the Park staff for answering questions and assisting me whenever I needed help.

I would also like to acknowledge the Park personnel who have over the years documented the Park's development in photographs. Some of the names that reoccurred as the man or woman behind the camera were John Stockert, Susan Sindt, J.J. Palmer, W. Bryant, G. Watzel, Jack Boucher, R.A. Grom, Lloyd Fletcher, E.J. Bucknail, and R. Sims. Without their dedication, an important part of Park history would have been lost.

I was constantly in search of old photographs of the homesteading and ranching days. I am indebted to local residents for finding pictures for me. Thank you to Wanda Guptill for sharing her wonderful rodeo collection with me as well as locating pictures of Interior. My quest for pictures of the ghost town Conata led to Betty and Lawrence Kruse, who graciously shared their photos of Conata as well as interesting stories. Also, thank you to Jan and Lyle O'Rourke and Bernice and Grady Crew for their photo contributions.

Under certain conditions, a place becomes part of us; we own it. We absorb it into our lives. It cannot be taken from us. It is ours, without title or deed.

—Alfred Lambourne

INTRODUCTION

For centuries the sun has risen over the banks of the White River, awakening an age-old land. Weathered, chiseled formations have stood rigid, outlined in the morning sun. They have appeared serene, almost reverent as they harbored ancient secrets within their colored bands of strata. Erosion has exposed their mysterious past.

The history of the Badlands can be traced back to approximately 77 to 80 million years ago when the area was an inland sea during the Late Cretaceous epoch. Since that time, Badlands history and its inhabitants have progressed from the simple sea creatures that flourished. Eventually the seas drained away leaving thick sediments. The uplifting of huge landmasses followed. About 65 million years ago the Black Hills were formed as a result of this uplifting. The rivers flowed east to the Badlands leaving behind more deposits of sediments, which began to build layer upon layer. Unusual animals that followed the extinction of the dinosaur populated this tropical climate of the Eocene and Oligocene era. These new breeds of animals consisted of mammalian oreodonts as well as small horses and camels, ruminating animals resembling pigs, several types of rhinoceros, saber-toothed tigers, and the protoceras. Animals that died during the hot wet Oligocene epoch were covered with sediment.

The Oligocene epoch lasted approximately 11 million years. Then, volcanic eruptions took place in the western part of the continent, spewing forth ash that was carried by winds and streams to be eventually deposited in the Badlands. The climate changed and the oreodonts, titanotheres, and other Oligocene animals died.

Erosion began to wear away at the two thousand feet of sediment that was deposited over 30 million years. Wind, water, and frost eroded the clay formations, eventually carving the intricate pinnacles, saw-tooth ridges, and natural bridges and in the process, exposed fossilized bone.

Two million years ago sheets of ice moved across part of North America, however, the glaciers did not reach the Badlands. Mastodons, well suited to the colder climate, roamed the Badlands and were later replaced by the mammoths when the weather became warmer. Archaeologists have discovered evidence of early man hunting mammoths on the southern edge of the Badlands.

Over time, a semi-arid climate developed, leaving little water in the area. A different type of animal inhabited this sparsely vegetated place. The bison, pronghorn, bighorn sheep, wolf, coyote, and rattlesnake were among the many species that could tolerate the extreme temperature changes and the sparse existence of water or lush vegetation.

Archeological sites have revealed that prehistoric Indians occupied the area. Research tells us that they came to hunt and then to return to their villages along the rivers. Darkened, fire cracked rocks, and charcoal have tumbled down the eroded hills from exposed fire pits once dug into the earth to cook the bison or other game they had hunted with their spears and arrows. Potsherds and broken bison bones collected at these sites reaffirm early human occupation.

In the late 1700s, the Teton Sioux, driven from the east, moved into the area from Minnesota. With the acquisition of the horse, they became mobile and did not stay in one place long. They named this region with its craggy formations and deep canyons, "Mako Sica," meaning Land Bad. They only used the Badlands as a passage way from one place to another. They did not relish journeying through it and avoided this semi-arid region with little water and steep slopes whenever they could.

French fur traders passing though the Badlands agreed with the Indian's assessment. They called this area "les mauvaises terres a traveeser" (bad lands to travel across). Fur traders noticed, as early as 1834, a graveyard of bones strewn across the terrain. They told of these unusual fossils and brought samples back to the trading centers. It wasn't until 1840 that scientists began a serious inquiry to determine the origin of the strange bones. Despite Indian protests, many expeditions traveled to the Badlands, carting away wagonloads of fossils.

After the Indian wars for control of western South Dakota ended and the near extinction of the bison, their major source for food, the Sioux were placed on reservations. The surplus land between the White and Cheyenne Rivers was opened for settlement in 1890. Cattlemen, some of them foreign investors, used the public domain to range cattle. No fences contained them and they drifted for great distances.

Most homesteaders flocked to the surrounding area of the Badlands after the railroad crossed the Missouri River in 1906 in hopes they could prove up on 160 acres of land. Life was hard in this area that received 14 inches of annual rainfall or less. Later, during the drought years of 1910–1911 many left, leaving behind a trail of dust as they backtracked to the east. During the drought and economic depression of the 1930s, even more fled, selling their homesteads to the Resettlement Administration. Some of the purchased land would be included in the proposed national park.

The large cattle empires, edged out by the homesteader and their fences, also succumbed to the severe winter conditions, the drought, and the Great Depression. Small cattlemen adjusted their methods for stock raising and found a way to hold on.

Peter Norbeck, a South Dakota congressman, had a vision when he visited the Badlands in 1911 that one day it would become a national park. He knew this semi-arid land would not sustain agriculture and the extensive fossils reserves would be lost if not protected soon. He worked with his friend Ben Millard and others for many years overcoming obstacles to achieve his goal. Unfortunately, he did not live to see the Badlands designated as a national monument in 1939 or as a national park in 1978.

The Badlands is a unique phenomenon, covering 244,000 acres in three South Dakota counties. Its geological grandeur, fossil reserves, wildlife, and history will be protected for future generations under the supervision of Badlands National Park.

One

THE FOSSIL HUNTERS

O wilderness of drifting sand,
O lonely caravan!
The desert heart is set apart,
Unknown to any man.

—Walter Prescott Webb

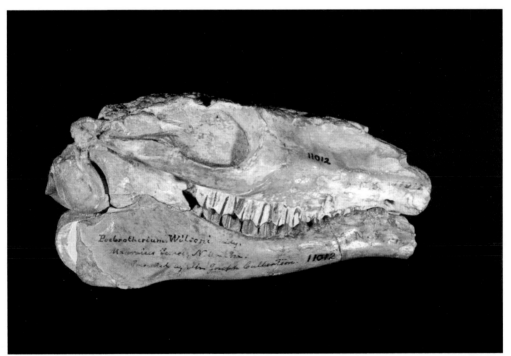

Early trappers and traders were the first to report of the Badland's unusual terrain and the strange bones found there. Scientific expeditions to the region were organized to investigate these reports. Dr. Joseph Leidy of Philadelphia, credited with the second scientific report filed, described this fossil of a prehistoric camel that he found in the Badlands in 1847. The fossil is on display at the Academy of Natural Sciences in Philadelphia.

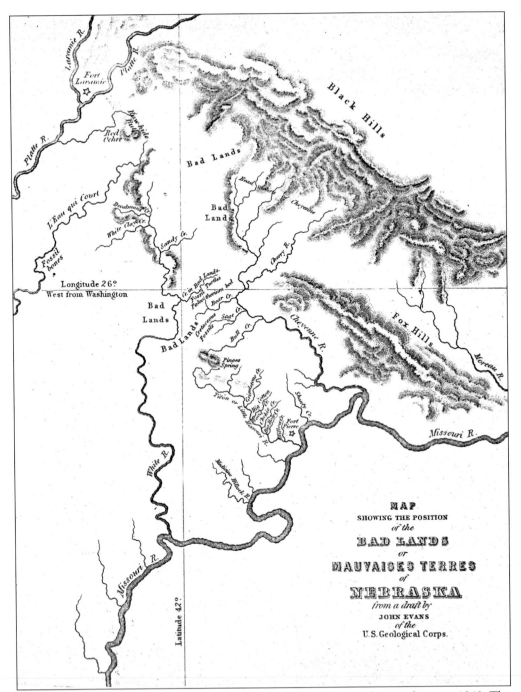

Dr. John Evans drew the first map of the Badlands while on a scientific expedition in 1849. The Badlands was a part of Nebraska territory at the time.

E. De Girardin, an artist for Dr. Evans scientific expedition, sketched the earliest published view of the White River Badlands in 1849. (Courtesy South Dakota School of Mines and Technology.)

De Girardin sketched the Evans expedition in the Badlands. He described the Badlands as an immense city in ruins and marveled at its architectural forms. His enthusiasm was dampened by the heat and the scorching sun of the near-desert environment. The expedition loaded their wagons with fossilized turtles, oreodonts, and other petrified bones. (Courtesy South Dakota School of Mines and Technology.)

The early fossil hunters, Alexander Culbertson, Dr. Evans, Fielding Meek, Ferdinand Hayden, and others, hauled away cartloads of fine specimens. The fossilized turtle above is one example. Many of the fossils are on display in museums all across the country.

In 1850, Thaddeus Culbertson, the younger brother of Alexander, visited the Badlands under the auspices of the Smithsonian. Although in awe of the scenery, he was initially disappointed with the fossil specimens. Instead of finding well-preserved skeletons, he found crumbling turtles as the one pictured above. Soon afterwards, he did find teeth, jawbones, and several skulls of animals.

Dr. Ferdinand Hayden, a renowned geologist, led many expeditions to the Badlands. The Sioux were not in favor of the white man's intrusion, but Hayden took the risk of their hostility. Because of the necessity of hasty collecting, the Sioux called Hayden, "He Who Picks Up Rocks Running." (Courtesy South Dakota School of Mines and Technology.)

The School of Mines and Technology made many early scientific expeditions to the Badlands. (Courtesy South Dakota School of Mines and Technology.)

The paleontologist uses a pick to remove unwanted rock around the exposed fossil. A preservative is applied to harden the fossil so that it can be removed without crumbling. Early scientists used a glue water mixture.

Fossils often erode out of hard to reach places. Dave Parris, in the dark cap, and an unidentified man are excavating a fossilized giant pig jaw.

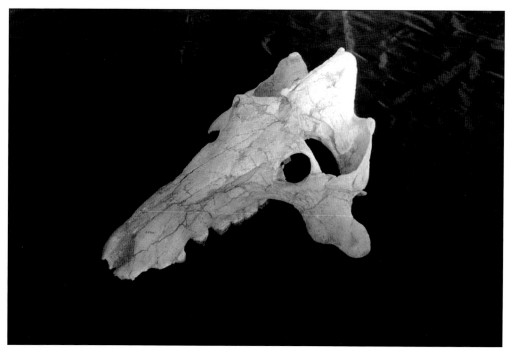

A fossil of the upper jaw of a giant pig dates back to the Oligocene epoch around 28 million years ago. The giant pig was a mammal about the size of a cow, which ate both vegetable and animal food.

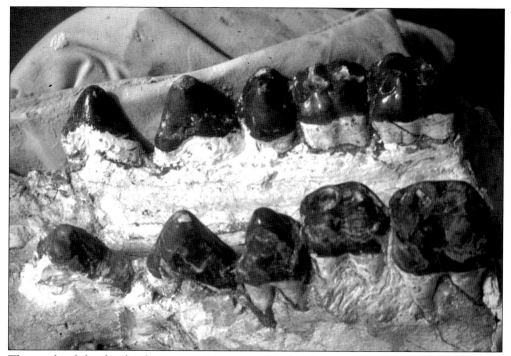

The teeth of the fossilized giant pig jaw appear black. The enamel of the teeth attracts the chemical manganese giving them their blue-black color.

The large fossil bone is of a titanothere, the largest known Badland's fossil. The titanothere was the same size as our present-day rhinoceros. The Sioux called these bones that they found thunder-horses.

Dr. John Clark investigates a small but concentrated titanothere fossil bone pile on the left edge of Sheep Mountain Table.

A fossil skull protrudes from the sun-baked clay at Norbeck flat.

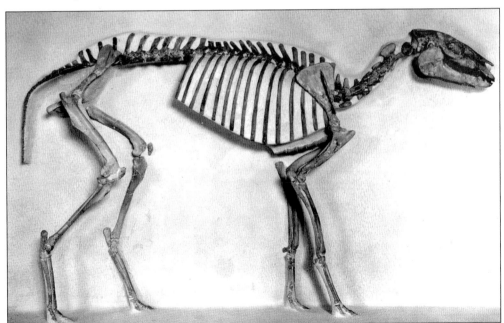
This skeleton on display at the School of Mines and Technology is of a three-toed horse. It had almost evolved to the present day horse when it disappeared from the Badlands.

An early form of saber-tooth tigers lived here during the Oligocene. The tiger's distinguishing characteristic was his saber teeth in the upper jaw, which he used to stab his prey. Because fossils are fragile, the archeologist carefully removes the specimen after it has been hardened with preservatives and coated with plaster.

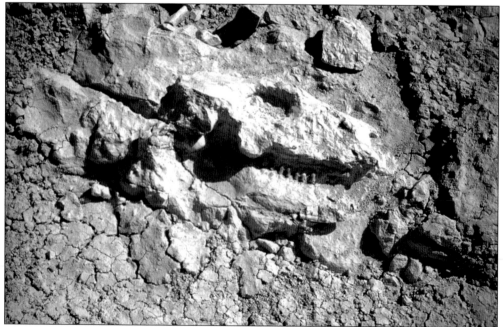

The most common fossil found is that of the oreodonts. They have been called ruminating pigs since their skeleton resembled a pig, but they chewed cud like a cow. There were 22 kinds of oreodonts that once lived in the Badlands almost 40 million years ago.

Two

NATIVE PEOPLES

Nature makes the man to fit his surroundings.

—Luther Standing Bear

Prehistoric Indians occupied sites such as this one atop Millard Ridge. Carbon dating indicates occupation between 896–1187 A.D. While watching for game, the men knapped stone tools. The women cooked food, made pottery, and prepared hides.

The late prehistoric Indians came from their homes along the Missouri River to hunt buffalo, deer, and antelope as well as to procure stones for tools. They chose sites such as Millard Ridge, overlooking the White River basin, to observe grazing animals.

Many fire pits, such as the one protruding from the Badlands, have been found throughout the area. The discovery of stone tools, flakes from flint knapping, bone fragments, bone tools, and potsherds have indicated prehistoric human occupation.

Fire pits eroding out of the Badlands provide charcoal for carbon dating. The pits were dug into the earth and lined with rock for cooking purposes. Some hearths measured by archeologists were 60 cm by 32.5 cm and 20 cm deep.

A fire was built in pits such as the one pictured, and allowed to burn down to a bed of coals. A layer of stones was placed over the hot coals and then the meat to be roasted was laid on the heated rock layer.

An archeologist collects charcoal from a fire pit for radiocarbon dating. Only organic materials can be used for carbon dating. The earliest site documented by radiocarbon dating in the Badlands is 2,500 years old. To date, five percent of the Park has been surveyed for archeological sites. Over 300 sites have been documented.

Dr. Dee Taylor from the University of Montana, kneeling to the far left, conducts archeological excavations near the Pinnacles overlook. Occupation sites at the Pinnacles spanned the time period 380 B.C. to A.D. 1650.

Arrowheads came into use when the bow and arrow was introduced in A.D. 500. On their hunting trips, Indians gathered various stones such as Badlands chalcedony, chert, and different colored quartz, all found west of the Missouri River, for making stone tools.

Cecil Lewis, to the left, stands along a crack on Millard Ridge in which an occupation layer shows up strong. Ten years later, archeologists would find a kill site on the southern edge of the Badlands. Fragments of two butchered Columbian mammoths and Clovis points were found suggesting occupation of humans to be much earlier.

A piece of pottery that the prehistoric Indians used has been reconstructed from pottery fragments. Archeologists believe the Indians may have made pottery at their summer hunting camps since pottery was too fragile to transport. Pottery pieces found at the Badlands are typical of pottery from the Initial Middle Missouri sites along the Missouri River.

The above is a sampling of artifacts discovered. The artifacts include a stone axe, projectile points, stone knives, a grinding stone, arrowheads, a stone drill, and potsherds.

This January 17, 1891 photo of Young Man Afraid of His Horse was taken in front of his tepee at Pine Ridge Agency. He was a prominent chief of the Lakota also known as the Teton Sioux. The Teton Sioux originated in the area of North Carolina and migrated into Minnesota and then South Dakota. They crossed the Missouri River around 1775. (Courtesy U.S. Signal Corps.)

Most of the Plains Indians sewed their dead in buffalo hides and placed them on scaffolds or in trees so the body could be near their creator. In early reservation times, people placed their dead in trunks left on top of the ground. This 1886 grave pictured was located at Black Pipe Creek and consisted of two trunks, a child's and an adult's. (Courtesy John A. Anderson Collection, Nebraska State Historical Society.)

Tepees line the horizon at a give away ceremony. Indian people brought gifts to be given away as thanks for a blessing, a special celebration, or to honor someone. The gifts, placed in the center of camp, were given away after a feast. (John A. Anderson Collection, Nebraska State Historical Society.)

After acquisition of the horse on the Great Plains, the Lakota left their woodland culture behind and became nomadic, following the buffalo as their means of subsistence. A woman scrapes the flesh from a pegged hide. Dogs used for beasts of burden in the early days provide companionship as well as food for a feast. (John A. Anderson Collection, Nebraska State Historical Society.)

The tepee was the dwelling place of the nomadic Sioux. Made from 15 to 18 buffalo hides sewn together with sinew and erected on a frame of poles, these tents could be taken down or be put up rather easily. Each tepee used about 20 poles that were set in a 15-foot circle. Three poles were tied together in a tripod with hide rope. The other poles were laid in the forks of these. (Courtesy Nebraska State Historical Society.)

In 1892, this would have been a typical Sioux encampment. Nearly 78 tepees made up this camp on the Pine Ridge Agency. Since the circle is a sacred symbol of the Lakota, the tepee was round and the encampment was set in a circular pattern. By 1883 nearly every family owned a wagon and team of horses. (Photo G. Trager, Nebraska State Historical Society.)

By 1890 the Lakota were relegated to reservations. The buffalo were gone and the government reduced rations. When they heard about the prophesies of Wovoka, a Pauite, their hopes of returning to their old life were restored. Wovoka's vision promised a new world where the earth would be reborn, abundant with buffalo and without the white man. Those who believed must dance the Ghost Dance. (Photo G Trager, Nebraska State Historical Society.)

Fearful of armed soldiers, who were instructed to stop the ghost dancing, supporters of the new messiah's vision fled to a natural walled fortress deep in the Badlands. This wide plateau, accessible only by a narrow land bridge, was known as Stronghold Table.

The Indians dug trenches on Stronghold Table that would enable them to hold off an encroaching army. Six hundred armed dancers brought enough food and livestock with them to last the winter. Their intention was to dance until spring, but the chiefs were persuaded to disband. On December 27, 1890 the last of the Ghost Dancers departed.

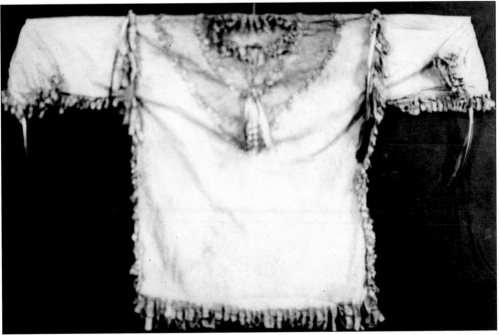

Made of muslin or cotton, the ghost shirt was adopted by the Lakota with the belief that it would be impervious to bullets. All men and women wore these holy shirts or dresses when they danced. The shirts were painted with different symbols. Usually an eagle was painted on the back, and eagle feathers were tied on the shoulders and sleeves.

This 1913 view of Big Foot Pass was used by Chief Big Foot in 1890 when he descended with his band of Minneconjou Sioux to the valley floor below. Big Foot, then seriously ill with pneumonia, watched his people lower the wagons down the dangerous slopes. He was eluding soldiers, who eventually caught up with him and escorted the band to Wounded Knee Creek. The next morning, in an attempt to disarm them, a gun was discharged, resulting in the ensuing tragedy.

The Lakota had no choice but to give up the old ways. They built log houses, planted gardens, tended livestock, and sent their children to school.

Three

THE OPEN RANGE AND THE HOMESTEADER

Crowds were drawn to the West for reasons of personal adventure, or because the romantic legends of the West attracted them. People were drawn by the intangibles, the touch of the wind on their faces, a return to the simple elements of living.

—Edith Ammons Kohl

This 1885 photograph of a person traveling by horse and buggy in the Badlands typifies the mode of travel at the time. Crude trails followed passable areas in the Badlands.

Leonel Jensen stands in the ruts of the Fort Laramie–Fort Pierre Trail. Trappers and traders used the route to transport furs and supplies between the two forts in the years 1826–1859. When trading furs was no longer lucrative, the trail was used to haul freight.

When this area was open to settlement in the 1890s, cattlemen brought their cattle from Texas to graze the free range. The 1895 corral was used by some of these cattlemen for their longhorn cattle.

The scene depicts the corral and crew of cowboys on John Hart's ranch. John Hart had been a freighter in Nebraska City when he came to the Black Hills in 1879. He established a sizable ranch on Spring Creek.

The signatures of early cowboys, J. Hart and H. Bell, are two of the many names carved into the wall of a cave that was abandoned by an earlier homesteader. Richard Bobier dug the cave in 1916 for a cellar. He added an air vent and built an entrance doorway out of boards.

A simple stone marks the grave of six-year-old Grace Robinson, the daughter of a Quinn Table homesteader, Kelly Robinson. Grace died of pneumonia and was buried on the homestead. Years later, Hank Bell and Butch Pipel located the lost grave site for the family and marked it with the original headstone and added a small footstone. A faint "G" appears in the upper left hand corner.

The original remains of Olive Wyant's barn and corrals have weathered the ravages of time.

Cattlemen often pitched tents in the Badlands when they worked cattle far from the ranch headquarters. This photo was labeled Camp #3 at Cedar Pass, August 1913. (Courtesy Keith Crew family)

The gray wolf roamed the Badlands in great numbers and was destructive to livestock in the area. Cattlemen felt that wolves were especially vicious with their prey. Wolves would slash the cords in their victim's legs and sometimes would begin to eat the downed animal while it was still alive. Big cattle outfits employed "wolfers" to search out the wolves and destroy them. Pictured here is a "wolfer's" camp near Potato Creek. Courtesy South Dakota State Historical Society.)

Bud Dalrymple, shown with the wolves he shot, was a "wolfer" for the 6L Ranch. Dalrymple was an expert on the habits and behaviors of wolves. Possessing considerable knowledge, he wrote articles for magazines and a book about wolfing. Bud was also a photographer and a gunsmith. He lived west of Scenic with his wife Norah.

Two ladies, named Mabel and Norah, hold up a wolf hide from one of Dalrymple's catches. (Courtesy South Dakota State Historical Society.)

Thousands of cattle grazed in and around the Badlands in the late 1890s and early 1900s. Severe blizzards of 1904 and 1905 reduced the herds. Many cattle were driven by the storms over steep precipices to perish in the canyons below. (Courtesy South Dakota State Historical Society.)

These cowboys enjoyed a brief respite from their daily work. (Courtesy South Dakota State Historical Society.)

In the early 1900s, several thousand sheep ranged from Ft. Pierre to Rapid City. Mike Miller, Herman Jacobs, and an unidentified man tend to sheep belonging to Louis and George Johnson in the year 1907 or 1908. The sheep operations provided wool for empty freight wagons returning to Ft. Pierre. The sheepherder's wagon, in the background, served as living quarters as they followed the sheep.

Louis J. Jenson, leaning against the butte, stopped with his team of mules to dry out after a sudden rainstorm or a wet river crossing with his hired man, Bill Anderson in this 1912 photograph.

Cedar trees were used extensively for fence posts. This 1912 cedar post fence contains horses in the pasture.

A number 14 wire was strung from the top of Red Cedar Butte to the bottom of the canyon to demonstrate how the early settler lowered the cedar posts that were cut for fencing. The posts were stapled to the sloping wire. The impact knocked the staples free when the post reached the bottom. Many rusty staples have been found at such sites.

Ernest G. Bormann, dressed in western attire, homesteaded 12 miles southwest of Wall along the north rim of Sage Creek Basin in 1912. He wrote a book, Homesteading in the South Dakota Badlands, in 1912 telling of his experiences. He owned the only film camera for miles around and took pictures of the homesteading days.

Here, Bormann stacks sod around his shack to insulate the foundation from wind and snow. Claim shacks were notorious for being hot in the summer and cold in the winter. Bormann writes in his book that he soon learned the only way he could keep his supply of potatoes from freezing was to leave them behind the stove during the daytime and take them to bed with him at night.

Bormann never intended to earn a livelihood from homesteading. He only stayed long enough to prove up on his claim, gain title, and then sell out. Bormann sold his tarpaper shanty in 1915 for $15. It was later moved to a ranch north of Wall.

Ernest Bormann washed clothes with the typical washboard and a pan of water. He was lucky to have a spring only a half-mile away to supply his water.

Bormann peels potatoes inside his shack. Bachelor homesteaders had to learn to cook and according to Bormann, organized cooking and baking clubs during the dry years. He writes that he used his pancakes to cover knotholes in the wall and propped up the corner of his claim shack with a loaf of inedible bread.

Standing in front of their frame house in 1908 is the Louis Jensen family, Mary, Veona, Leonel, Louis (holding Homer), and Bertha. Louis tells of his first trip to the Badlands in search of land in the Eastern Pennington County History. He rode a bicycle to Chamberlain from Viborg in 1906. When it broke down, he followed the Milwaukee Railroad on foot as far west as Vivian. He cut across country, locating land between Bull Creek and Crooked Creek.

Mrs. Josh Sullivan stands next to her 1908 sod house. Her daughters Mary, Rose, and Eveline pose in the foreground. A water barrel, a common sight, sits next to the house.

Ernest Bormann took a picture of the Bruce place southwest of Wall in 1912. R.F. Bruce was a county commissioner of Pennington County. Bormann worked for Bruce occasionally.

In 1913, Ed and Alice Brown pose by their prairie dwelling with their granddaughter and neighbor's daughter for a snapshot. An abandoned claim shack was added in that year to the original sod dugout home of 1909. The homestead was restored in 1962 by Dorothy and Keith Crew and is now on the National Register of Historic Places.

Pictured in front of their 1908 sod house are Marius Hutmacher, his wife Elizabeth holding Agnes, and Elizabeth's sister Mamie with Helen. Originally from The Netherlands, Marius filed on a claim near Scenic and later purchased the land for 50 cents an acre. He was periodically absent from his claim in search of work to support his family. The 1910–1911 drought drove them off their land. They relocated to Iowa. (Courtesy Kathy Getson.)

Claude Crew sent this postcard, dated July 12, 1909, from Interior to his parents, Ed and Lucy, in Pierce, Nebraska to let them know he had made it to the Badlands. He liked the Badlands so well that his parents, brother Leslie and sister Laura soon followed. The postcard reads: "Let me show you the trick, and he took her hand. For the one I love, I could split my land." (Courtesy Keith Crew family.)

Ed and Lucy Crew established their ranch two miles east of the northeast entrance to the Badlands. Many people stopped by the ranch for a visit on their way to a day of sight seeing and picnics. The Crews also hosted government officials who were locating the best route for the Park road. (Courtesy Keith Crew family.)

This early Cedar Pass road was not much more than a trail—rough, steep, and narrow at best. Rain made it slick and impassable. Horses pulling wagons would often fall to their knees on the uphill climb. Wagons had to be rough locked on the descent with logs or chains.

In about 1908, the township took the responsibility of building the Cedar Pass road over the wall to the northeast. The road was even trying for automobiles. Because early automobiles weren't equipped with fuel pumps and depended on gravity flow, cars often had to back up steep hills to distribute gas to the engine. Photo *c.* 1917–1918.

This 1912 bridge spanned the canyon near the top of Cedar Pass.

J.O. Hamm stands amidst the cactus in the vicinity of his well on a hot summer day in 1939. Water was a difficult resource to locate in the Badlands and was often alkali.

A farmer demonstrated his steel lug wheel tractor while plowing on Sheep Mountain Table in the early 1930s. This decade was plagued by drought and wind that removed the topsoil from the plowed field causing massive dust storms. Many homesteaders and ranchers sold land to the government during these hard times. Some of the land was added to the Badlands National Monument.

Four

SETTLEMENTS

When the railroad met the buffalo, the Iron Age met the Stone Age,
the machine arrived in the garden, and the West was changed forever.

—T.H. Watkins

An automobile descends the old Cedar Pass roadway in 1917. Ten years later representative citizens of Interior traveled to Pierre to see about an improved road.

About two and a half miles from present Interior; the first settlement in the Badlands was established as a trading post in 1889. The post office was named Black in honor of Phil and Barney Black's father, a settler in the area. After the railroad arrived in 1907, the town moved to the present location and was named Interior; *c.* 1906.

The Chicago, Milwaukee, and St. Paul Railroad extended its lines westward through the Badlands. In 1907, it reached the present site of Interior. Because of the railroad, Interior became a major shipping point for cattle and grain.

Standing in front of Johnson's General Merchandise Store in 1910 are Herman Jacobs, Lena Johnson, George Johnson, G.M. Brown, Judge Stover, John Evertt, Louis Johnson, Homer Drew, and Paul Olsen. In the fall of 1940, the store followed the fate of many buildings and burned to the ground.

The Johnson's General Merchandise Store was well stocked with supplies that the settler and rancher would need. From left to right the people pictured are George Johnson, Sam Petit, and John Ellingson; c. 1909.

In 1909, the town of Interior was bonded for $5,000 to install a water system. Pipes were laid in hand-dug ditches to pipe water from wells dug near the White River. A water tank was built and by July 10, 1910, Interior had the only water system between Murdo and Rapid City.

The mail carrier, E.A. Woodburn seated in the car, is ready to begin his route in Interior. Standing near him are Mrs. H.C. Snodgrass (banker's wife), Lena Johnson, Louis Johnson, and Erie Moore; c. 1920.

Interior was anticipated to be one of the most promising towns between Murdo and Rapid City.

A cowpoke saunters along the quiet streets of Interior in 1921. Interior had its social events that livened up the town. Potluck suppers, dances, and box socials were held in the town hall. Annual carnivals and three-day rodeos brought entertainment to the local area.

Over the years the business district grew to include two general stores, a butcher shop, hardware store, drug store, two hotels, café, barber shop, pool hall, saloons, confectionary store, stationery store, and five cream stations; c. 1928.

Interior also had two lumber companies, mortuary, blacksmith shop, feed store, livery stable, and two garages. In 1939, a major fire destroyed most of the business district from which it never recovered.

The brick schoolhouse built in 1910 stands to the left of the water tower. It was torn down in 1956. The Presbyterian Church looms to the right.

Calhoun's Garage was one of the many businesses that lined the street in the 1920s. A Hupmobile and a Stanley Steamer provided taxi service to the town.

In 1919, the first three-day rodeo, or round-up was held. The railroad sent out special rail cars as far as Chicago to bring tourists to the annual event. (Courtesy Jan and Lyle O'Rourke.)

Lloyd Coleman rides the bronc, Whisper. Spectators filled the grand stands for each three-day rodeo event. Chicago, Calgary, Cheyenne, and Belle Fourche were the first towns to establish an annual rodeo. Interior was the fifth.

Frank Hart, a local legendary cowboy, competes in one of the annual round-ups. (Rodeo photos courtesy of Wanda Guptill.)

The Oglala Sioux from the Pine Ridge Agency and the Sioux from the Cheyenne, Lower Brule, and Rosebud Agencies participated in Interior's round-ups. They took part in pony races, and the Medicine and Omaha dance.

Leonard Stroud demonstrates his ability as a trick rider at an Interior round-up during the 1920s. During competition, Leonard often combined trick riding and rope tricks that Will Rogers taught him. He was the first man to go under the belly of a running horse.

Dressed in full regalia, these Native Americans pose for a picture at one of the round-ups.

Anywhere from 300 to 500 Native Americans attended the round-ups each day.

The Native Americans held dances in the street during carnivals and round-ups. They brought tents and camped on the edge of town. Each day, local ranchers donated steers for them to butcher for food.

A Native American with a travois gives first aid to an injured rodeo competitor. Travois racing was also a part of the round-up competition.

The round-ups drew many talented rodeo people from around the nation. Kittie Canutt from Wallace, Idaho rode at the round-ups. She was known as the "Diamond Girl" because of her diamond studded tooth, which she was said to have removed and pawned when she needed entry money.

Mayme Stroud competes in trick riding for prize money. Entry fees were about ten dollars.

Myrtle Cox displays good form on "Two Face." Women competitors often designed and sewed their own costumes.

CHESTER BYERS CHAMPION TRICK, INTERIOR, SO.D.
(ROWBLEROY)

In 1969, Chester Byers was inducted into the Cowboy Hall of Fame. Will Rogers also taught Chester rope tricks.

KIRK GRAHAM ON "OVER THE TOP" INTERIOR, SO. DAK.

Kirk Graham entertains the spectators with his determination and skill to ride "Over the Top" to the finish.

62

Pictured are the judges at a round-up. They are Frank Craven, Johnie Mull, and John Craven.

Conata had two general stores. Two spinster sisters, Harriet and Bea DeHaan, owned one. Chris Heather owned the other. Conata was built by the railroad track west of Interior near the site of the Milwaukee Railroad's second reservoir. The area settlers obtained their water from the reservoir. The town eventually faded into a ghost town in the late 1940s. (Courtesy Lawrence and Betty Kruse.)

Conata area settlers pose for a picture. Pictured here, from left to right, they include Harry Barton, Sam Guieser, Henry Crawford, William Kruse, George Crawford, Harriet DeHaan, Lena Kruse, Mrs. Barton, Ann Kruse, Ruth Case, Clarence Meeks, Bertie Schuler, Joe Keliher, Con Scanlin, Hanna Kruse, Edith Kruse, Mrs. Rule, Bea DeHaan. Back row includes Robert Johnson, Anna Steffens, Mrs. Guieser, and John Ellingson. William and Lena Kruse were Lawrence Kruse's parents. Harriet, besides being the postmistress, was also the proprietor of the general store along with her sister Bea DeHaan. Anna Steffens was a woman homesteader who drove a single buggy over the Badlands to give aid to the sick. Clarence Meeks ran a horse ranch and lived in a dugout. (Courtesy Lawrence and Betty Kruse.)

Five

THE PARK ROAD

*Again and again the impossible problem is solved when we see that the problem is only a tough decision
waiting to be made.*

—Robert Schuller

Two well-dressed men, standing beside their grand autos, look over the Badlands with binoculars.
They may have been inspecting the Badlands for national park status. Peter Norbeck, a South
Dakota congressman envisioned that one day the Badlands would become a national park. He
worked diligently toward that goal for most of his life.

Pictured is J.R Richardson, surveyor for the construction of Monument Highway U.S. 16A. The state of South Dakota was required to build a road along the Badlands Wall before the Badlands could become a national monument by presidential proclamation; c. 1927.

J.R. Richardson began surveying for the park road in 1928. Much to Peter Norbeck's and his friend Ben Millard's displeasure the proposed road would miss the scenic heart of the Badlands. Both men explored and mapped out the most scenic route with the help of others.

Ben Millard built a dance hall on land that his sister Mrs. Jennings had purchased at the foot of Cedar Pass for a tourist development. The building was constructed of bark covered board slabs. Millard hired bands to provide music for dancing, drawing in people as far away as Rapid City. Lawrence Welk and his bands played here on occasion. The building also had a kitchen, dining room, and curio shop; c. 1929.

Pictured are Curly Nelson's wife and Mrs. Clara Jennings. Mrs. Jennings was a sister to Ben Millard, the founder of Cedar Pass Lodge. Mrs. Jennings financed Mr. Millard; c. 1931.

Camps for the road construction crews were set up throughout the Badlands. This one was located at the Pinnacles tunnel construction; *c.*1932.

The construction crew paused for a picture after the Pinnacles tunnel completion. From left to right the members include Henry Hanson, Stanley Gould, Ruphert Harris, Henry Lampkie, Lester Swanson, an unidentified man, Howard Harris, and Alfred Schkerl; *c.* 1932.

Horses and scrapers were used on the road construction on the grade below Sheep Mountain in 1936.

This crew construction camp was located at Sheep Mountain; c. 1936.

This view shows the timekeeper's and tool house at Sheep Mountain.

Caterpillars work precariously on the steep slopes to build the Sheep Mountain canyon road in the southern unit of the Badlands.

Since Leslie and Jessie Crew's ranch was located along the main road to the Badlands, they opened a gas station and sold fuel as well as iced lemonade to the tourists during the hot summer days. Their son, Keith, is pictured on the horse. (Courtesy Keith Crew and family.)

This automobile approaches the upper tunnel constructed in 1938. There were 42 miles of graveled roads by 1935.

This was the west portals tunnel in 1938.

A slide at the Norbeck pass tunnel in 1939 alerts engineers to the danger of tunnel construction.

In 1939, WPA workers prepare for tunnel removal. Because of rockslides and the unstable conditions of the Badland's soil, the tunnels were short lived. One year after their construction, they were obliterated.

The Badlands National Monument became aware that the timbers supporting the tunnel roof were in poor condition and might collapse. Two thousand vehicles passed through it every day during the height of the tourist season. A 69 man crew tore the Norbeck tunnel down in 1939.

Ben Millard proposed that two units of tourist facilities should be provided, a larger facility at Cedar Pass and a smaller one at the Pinnacles on the west entrance to the Badlands. When the road was completed in 1935, he started a small development at the Pinnacles. Even though he campaigned for improved buildings, the Pinnacles development was a make-shift affair.

In 1937, Ben Millard bought the Cedar Pass Lodge from his sister. He expanded his business by building cabins for the concession personnel and later would provide cabins for tourists.

A gas station provided fuel and services for tourist traffic that traveled the scenic loop through the Badlands; c. 1939.

The Cedar Pass Lodge dining room provided meals for the tourists in 1939.

This early photo of the 1939 Cedar Pass development gives us an encompassing view of the service station and cabins.

Porches were added to the rustic cedar slab cabins in hopes they would improve the design.

This photo was taken in 1939 looking down from the top of Cedar Pass at the lodge development.

The new Badlands road provided access to the scenic beauty of the Badlands National Monument.

Works Progress Administration (WPA) workers undertook many construction projects in Badlands National Monument. All men are unidentified except for the second man from the right. He is Chris Heuther Jr.

The WPA was created under Franklin Roosevelt's New Deal to provide jobs. WPA workers appear to be gathering and disposing of Russian thistles, the only plant that thrived during the drought years of the 1930s.

Six

BADLANDS NATIONAL MONUMENT

No moral man can have peace of mind if he leaves undone what he knows he should have done.
—John Wayne

As early as 1909, the State Legislature requested that the U.S. Congress set aside the Badlands as a national park. Because Congress did not act on this resolution, Peter Norbeck decided to take up the cause and visited the Badlands in 1911. He faced many obstacles and did not live to see President Franklin Roosevelt proclaim the region of the Badlands as Badlands National Monument on January 25, 1939.

The Cedar Pass development expanded in 1950 and included the administration building seen in the distance.

Ben Millard made significant contributions to Badlands National Monument, first as the operator and owner of Cedar Pass Lodge and as a staunch supporter of Peter Norbeck. Ben Millard was given the tribute "The Father of the Badlands."

An unidentified man looks under the hood of a National Monument service vehicle parked in front of the Visitor Center and administration building; c. 1950.

The concession buildings at the Pinnacles operated until 1950 when they were closed down.

The dining car built in Philip by a carpenter was moved by truck to the Pinnacles Overlook location east of Wall. Curly Nelson operated the facility during the summer of 1931.

A friend of Ben Millard stands in the doorway of "The House By the side of the Road." This was the nicest cabin and was usually rented to the newly wed.

The administration building appears in the foreground. The brick building in the background was the old superintendent's residence; *c.* 1954.

In 1957, a cable was tied around the old office building in order to move it back in preparation for an enlarged parking area.

Director Harvey prepares to lift the first shovel full of dirt during the new Visitor Center groundbreaking ceremony. From left to right are Chief Naturalist Jim Godbolt, Don Guiton, Region II Director Goodrich, Elloween Saunders, Contractors Corner and Lee, Axline and Rosenberg from Washington D.C., and Superintendent George Sholly holds the umbrella.

Ground leveling took place on July 1958 for construction of the new Visitor Center.

One month later, concrete grade beams were poured for the new Visitor Center.

The building begins to take shape as the steel beams are erected.

A severe windstorm on November 5, 1958 rendered heavy damage to the new Visitor Center under construction. The west wall was pushed outward and the north wall was pushed inward.

Cornor, Howe, and Lee contracted the Visitor Center construction. This photo was taken one month after the building sustained heavy wind damage. The back view of the building is shown.

After occupation of the new Visitor Center, the old office building was moved in July 1959 to the middle utility area.

Juniper trees for landscaping were removed from the Pinnacles area and brought to the Visitor Center.

The new Visitor Center stands ready and waiting to welcome tourists. Nearly 663,246 tourists visited the Monument two years earlier in 1956.

The Visitor Center was dedicated on September 16, 1959. A Sioux dancer participates in the day's celebration.

A Rosebud Sioux dancer performs the Eagle Dance at the dedication. The Lakota reveres the eagle as a special messenger, a guardian of the Lakota nation's sacred hoop.

The Chief of the Rosebud Sioux participates in the festivities preceding the speech making.

South Dakota governor
Ralph Herseth gives an
address at the dedication.

The Visitor Center, photographed in 1960 by J.J. Palmer, offers a spacious area for displays, books, and information.

This aerial winter scene of the Visitor Center was taken by H.E. Carlson, Corps of Engineers.

R.A. Grom took this 1965 photo of the Visitor Center. Attendance to the Monument steadily increased yearly.

The Pinnacles Ranger station provided a needed service on the west end of the Monument during 1967.

The Oglala Sioux assumed administration of the concession in 1971. Left to right are Jerry Clark; Curley Nelson; Supt. Cecil Lewis; Elliott Halsey; and Gerald One Feather, Tribal President.

Photographed in 1976, the concession building continues to provide a gift shop, a restaurant, and tourist information.

In 1978, the Badlands were designated as Badlands National Park. Originally when Peter Norbeck conceived the idea of a park, he had proposed such names as Wonderland or Teton National Park, fearful that Badlands would impart a negative image.

Seven

FLORA AND FAUNA

The West is color. Its colors are animal rather than vegetable,
the colors of earth and sunlight and ripeness.

—Jessamyn West

During wet springs, wild flowers abound in the Badlands. The tufted evening primrose is one among many. Also called the gumbo lily because it grows on clay banks, this delicate white flower blooms after sunset, turns from pink to rose, and wilts before noon of the next day.

The prickly pear blooms from June through mid-July. Later, a fruit appears which the Indians ate after removing the bristles. The juice from the stem was used as a fixative to set the paint used on hides. They also used the peeled stems as a dressing for wounds.

Early settlers collected and dried cactus pads for fuel. They also placed the pads in murky water to settle it. When fruit for jelly making was in short supply, pioneer women removed the spines from the cactus fruit and prepared a jelly.

The prairie turnip, also known as the Indian turnip or tipsin, was used by the Sioux Indians for food. The women dug the bulbous roots in June or July to use in stews or to eat raw. They also braided and dried a supply for winter use.

Mary Margaret Stockert inspects a yucca, which can reach a height of three feet and produces bell shaped flowers. The yucca or soap weed was utilized by the plains tribes for multiple purposes. They used the root for soap, the sharp leaf points for needles, the fibrous leaves for thread or basket making. The Teton Sioux bound the pointed blades together for use as a fire drill.

The dainty blooms of the meadow rose appear on low thickets from May to July, gracing the spring breeze with their fragrance. The fruits, rose hips, were eaten when there was a scarcity of food. According to Sioux legend, Mother Earth wished for colorful flowers to brighten her prairie robe of drab gray. Granting her wish, a pink flower, the color of dawn light, sprung from Mother Earth's heart.

The rabbitbrush prefers the poor, dry soil of the Badlands, growing up to four-feet high. It blooms yellow from late August to October and provides forage for wildlife when other food is scarce.

Other than a few ponderosa pines, Rocky Mountain junipers or cedars are the only evergreen in the region. When the Teton Sioux were plagued by the Asiatic cholera epidemic in 1849–1850, Red Cloud tried a decoction of boiled cedar leaves. This was drunk and used for bathing.

The cottonwood tree grows in areas of sufficient moisture. Its lustrous leaves dance in the breeze making a rustling sound. Regarded as a sacred tree, the Sioux used a cottonwood pole as the central focus of the sun dance ceremonies. Young cottonwood branches provided forage for their horses. The Sioux boiled the buds to make a yellow dye. The children crafted toy tepees and toy moccasins from the leaves. Early settlers used the cottonwood for building.

The gray wolf once roamed the Badlands in great numbers. They were a threat to the livestock industry and were eliminated.

In 1861, a drought lasting for three years drove the bison out of the Badlands in search of grazing. The drought combined with over hunting of the bison, caused their decimation across the plains.

In 1963, bison were brought from Theodore Roosevelt National Park in North Dakota to eventually replace the herds that once grazed the area.

By 1970 the herd of bison increased to 400 free to roam 64,000 acres of Sage Creek and Tyree Basin.

Periodically, bison are brought into specially constructed corrals where they are weighed and vaccinated.

Bighorn sheep were reintroduced into the Badlands in January 1964 to replace the extinct Audubon sheep that once populated the Badlands in great numbers. They were hunted into extinction.

Bighorn sheep were released in a penned area where they had a chance to acclimate before they were set free.

A sure-footed Rocky Mountain bighorn sheep explores his new home away from the Rocky Mountains.

John Stockert photographed these bighorns in 1967, the third year after reintroduction.

The cliff swallow migrates to southern South America when the weather turns cold in the Badlands. It lives in colonies near cliffs where it can build its nests.

The cliff swallows' jug-shaped nests are clustered together under a cliff overhang.

A visitor found this golden eagle, apparently abandoned by its parents after falling out of a nest in June 1971. Susan Sindt took care of it until it could be released.

Two months after the eagle was found, Susan Sindt and Don Higgins released it in the Sage Creek Basin feeling confident that it could survive on its own.

The golden eagle, named for the golden brown feathers on the back of its head and neck, is just one of the many birds found in the Badlands.

This newly released eagle poses as if ready for its first flight. Soon it will open its wings into a seven foot-wing span enabling it to gracefully soar over the Badlands.

Eight

SCENIC WONDERS

The finest workers in stone are not copper or steel tools, but the gentle touches of air and water working at their leisure with a liberal allowance of time.

—Henry David Thoreau

N.H. Darton, a photographer for the U.S. Geological Survey, took some of the first scenic photographs of the Badlands. His photographs featured here were taken in the south unit of the Badlands National Park. Unfortunately, due to a century of erosion, some of these formations are now unrecognizable.

An unidentified man investigates the natural bridge in the protoceras sandstone area near the head of Corral Draw in this 1898 N.H. Darton photo. Many fossils of the protoceras, an unusual animal with five pairs of horns on its face, were found here.

This N.H. Darton photograph was taken in 1897 at the head of Indian Draw. The formations are protoceras sandstone.

N.H. Darton took this photograph in a divide at the head of Cottonwood Draw in 1901.

This 1901 photograph, taken by Darton in Indian Draw, is near extensive titanotherium beds. The titanotheres, the largest known Badlands fossil, were slightly smaller than today's elephant.

The Lakota Indians named this region "Mako Sica" meaning, Land Bad. The early French-Canadian trappers in this area in the late 1700s called it "les mauvaises terres" bad lands. Settlers referred to the region as "badlands." Water was scarce and hardly fit to drink and temperatures were extreme in summer and winter. The steep canyons and formidable Badlands Wall made travel difficult.

Dr. Hayden, a geologist, visited the Badlands in 1853. At first he was optimistic about the region referring to it as a paradise. Later he lamented in letters, "It seemed as if all nature animate and inanimate was against me to prevent the success of my efforts."

Many black and white postcards of the Badland's unique scenery were sold to tourists. The next five postcards catch a glimpse of the unusual formations.

James Clyman, a member of Jedediah Smith's trapping and trading expedition, is given credit for the earliest description of the White River Badlands. He noted the lack of vegetation in the region and the eroded knobs and gullies composed of a soil very soluble in water.

E. De Girardin, a French artist employed by Dr. Evan's expedition in 1849, was inspired by the Badland's beauty. He wrote an eloquent description of his observations. He, like many, described the Badlands as a "city in ruins" possessing bizarre architecture of embattled chateaus and pyramids. The pillars amidst the ruins appeared as a "gigantic light house," he said.

With some imagination, one can see a mighty dragon presiding over the landscape in this postcard.

Father DeSmet visited the Badlands in 1848. He described the landscape viewed from a distance as "extensive villages" and "ancient castles from some new world."

In 1859, the Smithsonian Institute arranged for Thaddeus Culbertson to visit the Badlands. He thought they resembled a large city. He went on to elaborate the he could imagine the formations resembling public buildings such as a town hall, a court house, and a row of palaces inhabited by giants.

Dr. Evans thought the Badlands offered a pleasing contrast to the "monotonous prairie." The valley "looks as if it had sunk away from the surrounding world," he said.

A scene such as this one south of Sheep Mountain inspired Captain John Todd, who accompanied the Harney expedition in 1855. In his journal, he described the scenery as "solitary, grand, chaotic, as it came from the hands of Him. . . ."

In 1890, the Western artist Frederic Remington accompanied a scouting party to the Badlands in search of Big Foot and his band. He said of his venture, "No words of mine can describe these Bad Lands. They are somewhat as Dore pictured hell."

117

Vampire Peak, located near Cedar Pass, was a landmark to early settlers; *c.* 1935.

John Stockert photographed Vampire Peak in 1968. Thirty-three years of erosion had altered the peak's appearance. The two fang-like spires had eroded away. The rate of erosion throughout the Park depends on soil composition. The spires on Vampire Peak were composed of consolidated ash so they eroded quickly.

Louis J. Jensen and a hired man take a ride in the buggy near Sage Creek Pass in 1914. (Courtesy South Dakota State Historical Society, Leonel Jensen Collection.)

Riders stop to gaze on the pristine Badlands. (Courtesy South Dakota State Historical Society, Burt Dunbar Collection.)

The Crew family and neighbors spend a day in the Badlands. Picnicking was a popular Sunday pastime. (Courtesy Keith Crew family.)

Visitors from the surrounding area enjoy an outing in the Badlands. (Courtesy Keith Crew family.)

A horse drawn buggy meanders up the steep, narrow Cedar Pass trail. (Courtesy Keith Crew family.)

The Badlands Wall provides a barrier between the upper and lower prairie. Its spires, peaks, and ridges made travel difficult.

The average elevation of 200 feet is the difference from the upper and lower prairie.

This is a section of the steep wall between Norbeck and Cedar Pass.

An aerial view shows the rough terrain of this seemingly impenetrable wall. The four major passes, Cedar, Norbeck, Dillion, and Big Foot render travel possible across this barrier.

Norbeck Pass was named for Peter Norbeck, who was instrumental in preserving the Badlands for posterity.

In 1965, 130,000 acres of the Pine Ridge Reservations was proposed as an addition to the Park. Park personnel look over the remote Palmer unit.

Earl A. Jones, a seasonal ranger, patrols Sage Creek Basin in the fall of 1956.

Streams have cut through the sediments deposited over millions of years, revealing the colored banded layers laid down during the late Eocene and Oligocene times.

Not all of the Badlands National Park is composed of ridges, gullies, and peaks. Sixty percent of the Badlands Park is covered by prairie. The photo was taken along the south fork of Sage Creek.

Sage Creek Basin is composed of extensive grasslands that support the bison, antelope, and a prairie dog town nearby.

The School of Mines Canyon plunges to depths of 100 feet. This photo was taken c. 1937.

Junipers and ponderosa pine grow along the rim of Sheep Mountain enhancing the area's natural beauty. Over 244,000 acres of grandeur are forever preserved as Badlands National Park.

BIBLIOGRAPHY

Freeman, Criswell, ed. *The Wisdom of the West*. Nashville, Tennessee: Walnut Grove Press, 1997.

Gilmore, Melvin R. *Prairie Smoke*. St. Paul: Minnesota Historical Society Press, 1987.

Hall, Philip. *Reflections of the Badlands*. Freeman, South Dakota: Pine Hill Press, 1997.

Hauk, Joy Keve. *Badlands, Its Life and Landscape*. Interior, South Dakota: Badlands Natural History Association, 1968.

Mattison, Ray and Grom, Robert. *History of Badlands National Park*. Interior, South Dakota: Badlands Natural History Association, 1968.

Shuler, Jay. *The Revelation Called the Badlands, Building a National Park 1909–1939*. Interior, South Dakota: Badlands Natural History Association, 1989.